Earth

Quinn M. Arnold

CREATIVE EDUCATION
CREATIVE PAPERBACKS

seedlings

Published by Creative Education and Creative Paperbacks
P.O. Box 227, Mankato, Minnesota 56002
Creative Education and Creative Paperbacks
are imprints of The Creative Company
www.thecreativecompany.us

Design by Ellen Huber; production by Joe Kahnke
Art direction by Rita Marshall
Printed in the United States of America

Photographs by Alamy (Dmitry Rukhlenko - Photos of India,
Science Photo Library, Johan Swanepoel, Zoonar GmbH), Corbis
(NASA), Dreamstime (Blackzheep), Flickr (Derek K. Miller/
Flickr/NASA), Hubble Collection (NASA, ESA, and the Hubble
Heritage Team [STScI/AURA]-ESA), NASA (ISS Crew/Earth
Sciences and Image Analysis Lab/JSC), Pixabay (Comfreak,
skeeze), Science Source (Richard Bizley, Detlev van Ravenswaay),
Shutterstock (bazzlewazzle, biletskiy, leonello calvetti, Manuel Breva
Colmeiro, Imagine Photographer, Merydolla, Seaphotoart, Johan
Swanepoel, TinnaPong)

Library of Congress Cataloging-in-Publication Data
Names: Arnold, Quinn M., author.
Title: Earth / Quinn M. Arnold.
Series: Seedlings.
Includes bibliographical references and index.
Summary: A kindergarten-level introduction to the planet
Earth, covering its orbital process, its moon, and such
defining features as its clouds, oceans, and forms of life.
Identifiers: ISBN 987-1-60818-913-7 (hardcover) / ISBN 987-1-
62832-529-4 (pbk) / ISBN 987-1-56660-965-4 (eBook)
This title has been submitted for CIP
processing under LCCN 2017938958.

CCSS: RI.K.1, 2, 3, 4, 5, 6, 7;
RI.1.1, 2, 3, 4, 5, 6, 7; RF.K.1, 3; RF.1.1

First Edition HC 9 8 7 6 5 4 3 2 1
First Edition PBK 9 8 7 6 5 4 3 2 1

TABLE OF CONTENTS

Hello.

Earth!

Earth is the third
planet from the sun.

It is blue, green, and brown. Earth is both hot and cold. White clouds form in its skies.

Earth has large oceans.

People and animals live on Earth. Plants grow in its soil.

A moon orbits Earth.

Astronauts landed on Earth's moon in 1969. They collected dust and rocks to study.

It takes Earth
one year to go
around the sun.

The sun is what makes life on Earth possible.

Astronomers study planets. They look for signs of life in outer space.

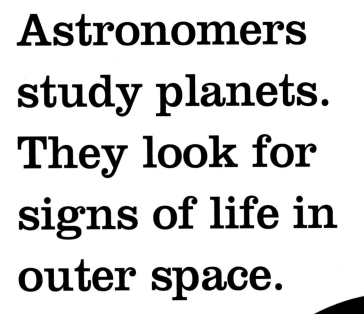

Winds blow white clouds. Waves crash onto land. Day and night come and go.

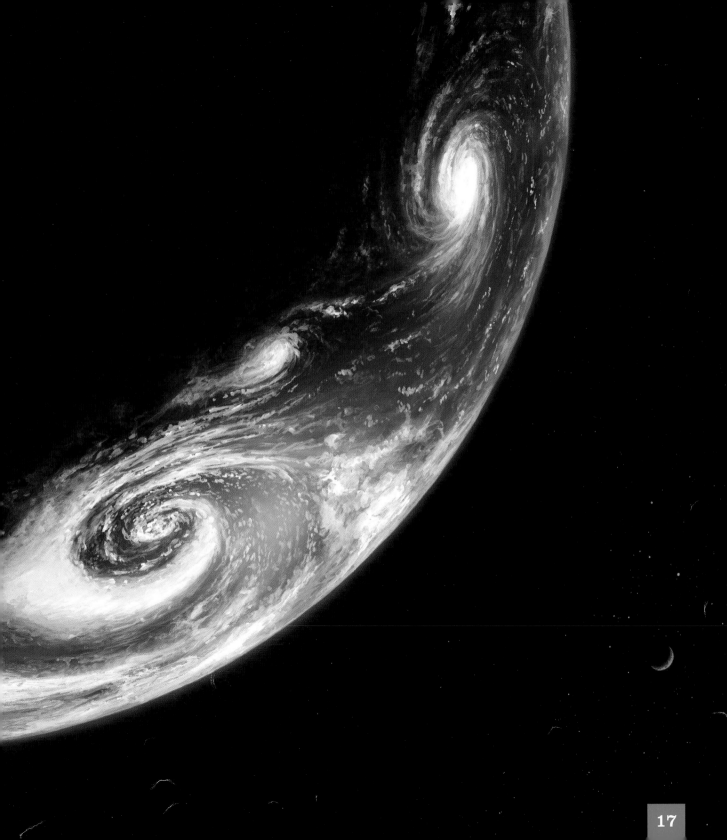

Goodbye, Earth!

Picture Earth

ice cap

atmosphere

ocean

clouds

cities

land

moon

Words to Know

astronauts: people who are trained to travel in outer space

oceans: big areas of deep, salty water

orbits: follows a path around a planet, moon, or other object in outer space

planet: a rounded object that moves around a star

Read More

Adamson, Thomas K. *Do You Really Want to Visit the Moon?*
Mankato, Minn.: Amicus, 2014.

Loewen, Nancy. *Our Home Planet: Earth.*
Minneapolis: Picture Window Books, 2008.

Websites

NASA Space Place: Earth
http://spaceplace.nasa.gov/menu/earth/
Watch videos, do activities, and play games to find out more about Earth!

National Geographic Kids: Mission to Earth
http://kids.nationalgeographic.com/explore/space/mission
-to-earth/#earth-planet.jpg
Learn how Earth moves through the solar system.

Index

moon